# Documenting the Cultural Heritage

Editors
*Robin Thornes*
*John Bold*

Council of Europe • Getty Information Institute • European Foundation for Heritage Skills

The Getty Information Institute
1200 Getty Center Drive, Suite 300
Los Angeles, California  90049-1680
Internet (World Wide Web):  http://www.gii.getty.edu

Design:  James Robie Design Associates
Printing:  Typecraft Lithography

ISBN 0-89236-543-9

# Contents

v     Foreword—Council of Europe

vii    Foreword—Getty Information Institute

ix     Acknowledgements

1      Introduction

13     The Standards

13         The Standards in Practice—The Example of Greenwich

27         Core Data Index to Historic Buildings and Monuments of the Architectural Heritage

33         International Core Data Standard for Archaeological Sites and Monuments

45         Object ID

49     Appendix:    Theoretical Framework of the Core Data Standard for Archaeological Sites and Monuments (with Glossary of Terms)

53     Notes

55     Bibliography

In fulfillment of its aim of achieving a greater unity within member states in order to safeguard their common heritage and to facilitate economic and social progress, the Council of Europe has for more than 25 years pursued a vigorous programme of cultural co-operation and celebration. High-level political debate within the European Conference of Ministers has led to the adoption of a number of key texts and associated recommendations. In the field of cultural heritage these have been translated into practical programmes of technical consultancy, assistance, training, and raising of public awareness. Through its own experience and through being able to draw on an enormous resource of accumulated expertise within the member states, the Council of Europe is uniquely equipped "to help national, regional and local authorities to tackle complex issues of enhancing, managing, and preserving the cultural heritage in an integrated way."[1]

To move from questions of principle to issues of practical application, it is essential to act within a framework of agreed guidelines and standards that are allowed to evolve through changing times and circumstances. Such a framework carries with it the authority achieved through consensus and enables individual countries and organisations to move forward on the basis of commonly agreed assumptions and conclusions, avoiding the need for the re-invention of solutions to settled questions. As the number of states that have acceded to the European Cultural Convention has grown to over 40, it has become more and more necessary not only to promote common values in the management and enhancement of the cultural heritage but also through cultural co-operation to provide the common mechanisms that allow us to preserve, celebrate, and enrich that heritage for the benefit of those who follow. Accurate documentation is fundamental to this task.

José María Ballester
*Head of the Cultural Heritage Department*
*Council of Europe*

In recent years there has been a growing recognition of the benefits of creating cultural heritage information networks that will enable common access to documentation created and managed by divers organisations. An important precondition to the development of such networks is the documentation standards that establish the degree of compatibility needed to make common access possible. The Getty Information Institute has considerable experience in working collaboratively to develop documentation standards, guidelines, vocabularies, and other tools that improve access to information about the cultural heritage.

The Information Institute followed with interest the development of the Council of Europe's Core Data Index to Historic Buildings and Monuments of the Architectural Heritage, and was pleased to co-operate in the running of follow-up training programmes in France (1995) and England (1996). It has also taken a close interest in the development of the International Core Data Standard for Archaeological Sites and Monuments, participating in a number of meetings of the Archaeological Sites Working Group of the Documentation Committee of the International Council of Museums (ICOM/CIDOC). For its part, the Institute would like to thank the Council of Europe for its assistance in developing Object ID, the recently established international standard comprising the information required to identify cultural objects.

The Institute is pleased to be associated with the Council and the European Foundation for Heritage Skills in producing this publication, which will play an important part in encouraging the implementation of these key standards. The presence of accessible, high-quality cultural heritage information on emerging electronic networks can be ensured only by the willingness of organisations to work together to attain this common goal. The three initiatives presented here were produced in a spirit of collaboration between organisations and nations, and represent significant steps toward that goal.

Eleanor E. Fink
*Director*
*The Getty Information Institute*

The editors wish to acknowledge and thank the Council of Europe, the Getty Information Institute, the Inventaire Général, the Royal Commission on the Historical Monuments of England (RCHME), and the Documentation Committee (CIDOC) of the International Council of Museums (ICOM) for the invaluable institutional support they have provided in the development of the documentation standards described here. We are grateful to Daniel Thérond, who began these documentation and inventory activities within the Council of Europe and is now, as Director of the European Foundation for Heritage Skills, responsible for follow-up and implementation activities on behalf of the Council's Cultural Heritage Committee. For their fundamental work in the conceptualisation and realisation of the concept of core data, we are also indebted in particular to Simon Grant and Monique Chatenet.

For their work in the development of the individual standards, we would like to thank the following:

The group of specialists on architectural heritage documentation responsible for the Core Data Index to Historic Buildings and Monuments of the Architectural Heritage, and in particular Monique Chatenet (France), Simon Grant (UK), and Olivier Toche (France); for facilitating discussions and encouraging positive conclusions, Daniel Thérond (Council of Europe); and for significant procedural contributions, Isabelle Balsamo (France), John Hume and Roger Mercer (UK), Jean Vincent (France), and Walter Wulf (Germany).

The Archaeological Sites Working Group, and in particular Valetta Canouts (USA), Dominique Guillot (France), Henrik Hansen (Denmark), Roger Leech (UK), Judy Marsh (Canada), Gillian Quine (UK), Stephen Stead (UK), Irina Oberlander-Tarnoveanu (Romania).

All those who contributed to the development of Object ID, and in particular José María Ballester (Council of Europe), Maria Papageorge Kouroupas (U.S. Information Agency), Elisabeth des Portes (formerly of ICOM), Lyndel Prott (UNESCO); for identifying the need for the standard and initiating the project,

Eleanor Fink (Getty Information Institute); for their work in managing the project, Marilyn Schmitt and Cynthia Scott (Getty Information Institute); and for coordinating the contribution of the working group of conservation specialists, Margaret Mac Lean (Getty Conservation Institute) and Suzanne Deal Booth (consultant to the Getty Trust).

For their assistance with the compilation of the sample records, we thank Paul Pattison and Ann Robey of the Royal Commission on the Historical Monuments of England, and Jonathan Betts and Roger Quarm of the National Maritime Museum, London. We are grateful to the National Maritime Museum, London, for the provision of photographs of objects in their collection.

This publication presents three internationally agreed standards for the documentation of the cultural heritage: the Core Data Index to Historic Buildings and Monuments of the Architectural Heritage, the International Core Data Standard for Archaeological Sites and Monuments, and the recently agreed core data standard for identifying cultural objects—Object ID. These standards have been brought together in a single publication to provide a readily accessible guide for use by those responsible for documenting the archaeological, architectural, and movable heritage. The publication explains the genesis of the individual standards, presents each in turn, and provides examples of their application—examples that illustrate the compatibility of the standards and demonstrate the potential for linking them in documentation centres.

### The Importance of Documentation

The role of inventories in the management of the cultural heritage has long been recognised. They are indispensable, for purposes of identification, protection, interpretation, and physical preservation of movable objects, historic buildings, archaeological sites, and cultural landscapes. They have a significant place in all the major international conventions relating to the protection of the heritage.

The 1972 UNESCO Convention Concerning the Protection of the World Cultural and Natural Heritage included the provision that a World Heritage Committee be established, to which each party state would submit an inventory of its national heritage. Article 2 of the Council of Europe's Convention for the Protection of the Architectural Heritage of Europe (Granada, 1985) states that:

> For the purpose of precise identification of the monuments, groups of buildings and sites to be protected, each Party undertakes to maintain inventories and in the event of threats to the properties concerned, to prepare appropriate documentation at the earliest opportunity.[2]

Similarly, Article 2 of the Council of Europe's Convention on the Protection of the Archaeological Heritage (Valletta, 1992) requires each party to make provision for "the maintenance of an inventory of its archaeological heritage and the designation of protected monuments and areas."[3]

Inventories are also recognised as a vital weapon in the fight against the illicit trade in cultural objects. Article 5 of the 1970 UNESCO Convention on the Means of Prohibiting and Preventing the Illicit Import, Export, and Transfer of Ownership of Cultural Property called for the establishment and maintenance of national inventories of cultural property. In 1993 the Council of Europe, concerned by "the situation of the movable heritage in central and eastern European countries," organised an intergovernmental meeting in Prague. This meeting recognised:

> that the conservation and protection of the movable cultural heritage is currently amongst the worst problems facing central and eastern countries and agree that such problems can be solved through effective international cooperation in Europe within the framework of the Council of Europe, and in close cooperation with other international bodies, in particular UNESCO, the EUROPEAN UNION and INTERPOL.[4]

The meeting also stressed "how important it is to identify movable cultural property" and called for inventories to be compiled.[5]

The most recent major international initiative aimed at combatting the illicit trade in cultural objects is the 1995 UNIDROIT Convention on the International Return of Stolen or Illegally Exported Cultural Objects. This convention "seeks to create a unified code whereby claimants in countries that are party to the convention may sue in the courts of other signatory countries for the return of stolen or illegally exported cultural objects."[6] The importance of inventories is recognised by article 4, which states that the possessor of a stolen cultural object who is required to return it shall be entitled to fair compensation only if it can be proved that he or she

> exercised due diligence when acquiring the object. In determining whether the possessor exercised due diligence, regard shall be had to the circumstances of the acquisition, including the character of the parties, the price paid, whether the possessor consulted any reasonably accessible register of stolen cultural objects, and any other relevant information and documentation which it could reasonably have obtained.

### The Need for Documentation Standards

Organisations responsible for the cultural heritage are part of a network of mutual dependencies, needing to share information and maintain contact with fellow professionals in their own and associated fields. Information sharing is not only a prerequisite for the better understanding and effective management of the cultural heritage, but is important for other interrelated reasons, including:

- The promotion and interpretation of the heritage for vital economic purposes, such as cultural tourism and regional development,

- The reinforcement of cultural and social identity at regional, national, and international levels,

- The ability to combat the theft of and illicit traffic in cultural property on a global scale.

Although documentation of the cultural heritage is already carried out at local and national levels, the need to use information produced by documentation centres is becoming international in scale, responsive to global trends in economic activity, cultural awareness, and crime.

Now, with the possibilities that information technology offers for contact and information sharing, the benefits of creating cultural heritage information networks are clear: These include the enabling of common access to inventories created and managed by divers organisations. Common access can be achieved, however, only if documentation standards are developed to ensure compatibility between the databases that constitute the network. This compatibility is most readily achieved at the level of minimum or "core" information, i.e., those categories of essential, basic information common to a number of documentation projects. The adoption of such "core data" categories makes it easier to record, retrieve, and exchange information electronically. Although the concept of core data has been developed with computers in mind, it also has a wider application in representing a way of indexing, ordering, and classifying information, independently of whether that information is on paper, card index, or database. As a mechanism, it is not an end in itself, but is designed to provide a way in—a key—to further information held on a database or in an archive. Such further information will vary according to the needs and purposes of individual organisations.

The three initiatives presented in this publication have identified the core information regarded as necessary for documenting the architectural, archaeological, and movable heritage. The categories in all three have been drawn up, and approved by potential users, on the basis that they do not require organisations to collect information that they would not otherwise collect, or seek to make users conform to systems that are incompatible with their own needs. Rather, the core data categories provide agreed structures for the ordering of the information that is regarded as indispensable for proper cultural heritage management. Because they have been developed in similar ways, with comparable ends in view, the three standards presented here may either stand alone or, if organisational needs demand it, be linked together in order to make it possible to compile ensemble records of archaeology, buildings, and movable objects. In offering this possibility, they represent the achievement of a milestone in documentation, embracing both the movable and immovable cultural heritage.

The Core Data Index to Historic Buildings and Monuments of the Architectural Heritage (1992) was created to identify the categories of information necessary to record buildings of historic and architectural interest, and the International Core Data Standard for Archaeological Sites and Monuments (1995) to identify the categories necessary for documenting the immovable archaeological heritage. Object ID (1997) was developed to provide an international standard for the information needed to identify cultural objects, in response to the threat posed by the illicit trade in the movable heritage.

**Core Data Index to Historic Buildings and Monuments of the Architectural Heritage**

Article 17 of the 1985 Granada Convention requires parties to exchange information on "the possibilities afforded by new technologies for identifying and recording the architectural heritage." Taking its cue from the Convention, a roundtable was convened in London in 1989 to examine the tasks of architectural heritage information centres, the ways and means of improving co-operation between them, and the new technologies available to them in furthering their work. Among the recommendations of the meeting was the following:

> The standards relating to a minimum set of data elements and the technical specifications required for their communication should be identified. This should be done by determining which data elements are necessary for the recording of all buildings of historic and architectural interest in each state or institution for the furtherance of its own work; by determining how this data may be harmonised; and by setting standards for computer systems.[7]

A working group, with members drawn from heritage organisations in France, Germany, the Netherlands, Sweden, and the UK, was established under the aegis of the Council of Europe to identify essential data elements of a core record. In 1991 the group undertook a Survey of Architectural Inventories, one of the key aims of which was to establish consensus on the content of the proposed Core Data Index. Seventy-eight organisations in 26 countries, representing 137 inventories, responded to the questionnaire. The survey found that there was close agreement on the categories of information essential to any inventory of the architectural heritage.

In October 1992 the Council of Europe and Direction du Patrimoine (France) convened a colloquy in Nantes to discuss "Architectural Heritage: Inventory and Documentation Methods in Europe." The purpose of the meeting was to determine practical forms of co-operation between heritage documentation centres throughout Europe, and to prepare a definition of common standards based on a comparison of the inventory methods used in different countries. At the end of the colloquy, the participants—more than 150 from 24 countries—approved the Core Data Index prepared by the working group.

The analysis of the replies to the questionnaire survey, the discussions of the group of specialists, and the outcome of the Nantes Colloquy resulted in the drawing-up of a draft Recommendation. After approval by the Cultural Heritage Committee and the Council for Cultural Co-operation, the "Recommendation on the co-ordination of documentation methods and systems related to historic buildings and monuments of the architectural heritage" was adopted by the Committee of Ministers of the Council of Europe on 11 January 1995.

The basic aim of the Core Data Index is to make it possible to classify individual buildings and sites by name, location, functional type, date, architect or patron, building materials and techniques, physical condition, and protection status. It is not an end in itself, but a starting point—a key to further information held in databases, documentation centres, and elsewhere that is necessary for the detailed understanding and care of individual monuments.

The Index is designed to enable the compiler to make cross references to the more detailed information about a building, including written descriptions and photographs; associated archaeological and environmental information; details of fixtures, fittings, and machinery installed within individual buildings; and the information on persons and organisations concerned with its history. It is recognised that the needs for these deeper levels of architectural, archaeological, environmental, historical, and planning information will vary from organisation to organisation and country to country, and that each must define its own specific requirements. Figure 1 shows the relationship of the parts of the Index concerning each historic building and monument, while Figure 2 illustrates how the core record for a building or monument may be related to more comprehensive levels of information.

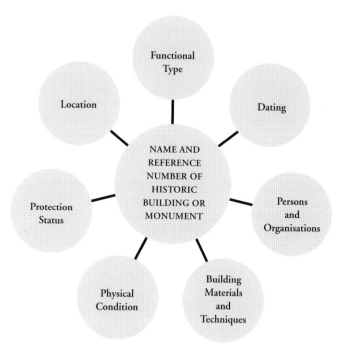

*Figure 1. Schematic representation of a record
structure for a building or monument*

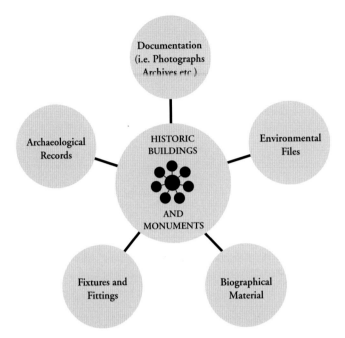

*Figure 2. Schematic representation of potential relationships between core monument records and related information*

The Index has the potential not only to record individual buildings, but also to enable the compiler to relate the building to a larger site of which it may be a component or to the still larger ensemble of which it may form a part. The architectural ensemble manifests itself in many different forms. It may be typologically or geographically defined. It may be planned or organic, unified or grouped by association, or united by a common functional purpose or community of interest. It may be based on the hierarchical relationship between a larger structure and its components, such as apartments in a house or the machinery in a factory. It may be spatial, involving the considerations of the relationships between buildings, the spaces between them, and the landscape in which they sit. Different cases and organisational priorities will result in ensembles being defined in varying ways according to circumstance, imposing cut-off points in different places, in order to make the material manageable and to allow the making of connections that will permit a more rounded view of the heritage.[8]

The Index does not seek to impose a rigid system, or to force organisations to act outside their own areas of interest. Nor does it seek to specify the computer hardware and software requirements of those organisations that are engaged in the process of computerising their information. Rather, it represents the first step towards defining and recommending technical standards for data capture and data exchange. It is possible to envisage a situation in which the mutual interrogation of indexed information will enhance our understanding of the architectural heritage of Europe. The Index is an important milestone on this road.

## Core Data Standard for Archaeological Sites and Monuments

The Core Data Standard for Archaeological Sites and Monuments is the result of a collaboration between the documentation committee (CIDOC) of the International Council of Museums (ICOM) and the archaeology documentation group of the Council of Europe. The standard has its origins in an international conference of representatives of national archaeological records held in Copenhagen in 1991.[9] At this conference it became clear that there were already many similarities between the approaches used for different national records, but that there was a need for closer co-operation in a number of areas, including that of documentation standards. The decision to develop a core data standard for archaeological sites and monuments was made at the 1992 CIDOC meeting in Quebec, and the Archaeological Sites Working Group was established to undertake the project. The aims of the group are as follows:

- To facilitate communication between national and international bodies responsible for the recording and protection of the archaeological heritage,

- To assist countries at an early stage in developing systems for the recording and protection of the archaeological heritage,

- To facilitate research utilising archaeological core data where this has an international dimension.

Shortly after the working group was established, the European Plan for Archaeology was launched under the aegis of the Council of Europe's Cultural Heritage Committee. The launch of the Plan, in April 1993, followed the signing of the revised European Convention on the Protection of the Archaeological Heritage at Valletta (Council of Europe, 1992) in January 1992, and was in accordance with Resolution 1 of the third Conference of Ministers responsible for the Cultural Heritage. One of the four main elements of the European Plan for Archaeology was a programme focusing on inventory and documentation techniques and standards with regard to the archaeological heritage. An important part of this programme was the preparation of a core data standard for records of archaeological sites and monuments, intended to complement the Council's Core Data Index to Historic Buildings and Monuments of the Architectural Heritage. When the Council of Europe working party became aware that the CIDOC working group was already preparing an archaeological data standard modelled on the Core Data Index, it decided that the most practical course of action was to adopt the CIDOC data standard as the basis of its own standard, subject to minor adjustments reflecting the narrower geographical focus of the Council of Europe.

In developing the standard, the working group recognised the importance of reaching a wide audience and involving archaeologists in as many countries as possible. From a small committee representing Canada, Denmark, France, Romania, and the UK, the group has expanded to include members from Albania, Brazil, Israel, Kenya, Madagascar, Poland, the Russian Federation, and the USA. There are also corresponding members in Germany, Jamaica, Latvia, the Netherlands, Norway, South Africa, and

Zambia. From the outset, the group undertook to ensure that its work was carried out in collaboration with other interested bodies, and there has been liaison with a number of organisations, including the Council of Europe, ICOMOS, the Getty Information Institute, and other CIDOC working groups. A questionnaire survey was undertaken to identify the contents of the standard. One hundred and nine responses were received from 35 countries, from organisations representing 177 individual inventories.

The International Core Data Standard for Archaeological Sites and Monuments of the Architectural Heritage has retained a close relationship with the Core Data Index to Historic Buildings and Monuments of the Architectural Heritage in order that countries wishing to include all information relating to the man-made environment on one database can do so. Moreover, the standard can be linked with other standards for movable objects, including the CIDOC standard for archaeological objects (1992), CIDOC's International Guidelines for Museum Object Information (1995), and Object ID (1997).

The standard was published in draft form in 1995 and circulated widely to heritage organisations. In September of that year it was discussed at a colloquy in Oxford organised by the Council of Europe and the Royal Commission on the Historical Monuments of England. The delegates to the meeting recommended that the standard be approved as part of the Council's European Plan for Archaeology.

The Core Data Standard has been designed to make it possible to record the minimum categories of information required to make a reasonable assessment of a monument or site, whether for planning, management, academic, or other purposes. In addition, it makes it possible to provide references to further information held in databases, documentation centres, and elsewhere that may be necessary for the detailed understanding and care of individual monuments or sites or categories of monument or site. It is also envisaged that the standard will:

- Provide a model that can be used as a framework by organisations wishing to establish new recording systems,

- Encourage consistency in the recording of archaeological sites and monuments,

- Function as an exchange format for the sharing of data,

- Form the basis of collaborative projects.

The authors of the standard recognise that different organisations record archaeological information for different purposes and to varying degrees of detail. For this reason, a number of sections, sub-sections, and fields are optional rather than mandatory, thereby allowing different organisations to record at a level appropriate to their aims and resources. The standard is intended for use in conjunction with the data model selected for the national or regional database. The data model will, in most cases, require modification to reflect the requirements of the organisation.

**Object ID**

The illicit trade in cultural objects is now widely recognised as one of the most prevalent categories of international crime. There is widespread agreement that documentation is crucial to the protection of cultural objects, since stolen objects that have not been photographed and adequately described are rarely recoverable by their rightful owners. However, it is one thing to encourage the compilation of descriptions of objects as a security measure, but quite another to develop effective means of circulating this documentation to organisations that can assist in their recovery if stolen. Ideally, the information that can identify a stolen or illegally exported object should be able to travel at least as fast as the object itself. This will mean that the information may have to cross national borders and be circulated among a number of organisations. The development of electronic networks makes this effort technically possible. But the existence of digital information and computer networks to transmit information solves only part of the problem; also needed are standards that will make it possible to exchange information in a form that is intelligible to both systems and people.

Discussions between the Getty Information Institute and leading national and international umbrella agencies and government bodies in 1993 established that there was a consensus on the need to collectively address issues relating to documentation practices and the implementation of international standards. In July of that year the Institute convened a meeting in Paris to discuss the possibility of developing an international collaborative project to define documentation standards for identifying cultural objects. The meeting was attended by representatives of the Conference for Security and Co-operation in Europe (now the Organisation for Security and Co-operation in Europe), the Council of Europe, the International Council of Museums, INTERPOL, UNESCO, and the U.S. Information Agency. The participants agreed on the need for such an initiative and recommended that it focus on developing a standard for the information required to identify cultural objects, and on the mechanisms for encouraging the implementation of the standard. As a result of these consultations, a project was defined and initiated, with the following primary objectives:

- To provide a collaborative forum for organisations that have demonstrated an interest in the protection of cultural objects,

- To recommend an international "core" documentation standard for the identification of cultural objects,

- To encourage the implementation of the standard.

From the outset, the project recognised the need to work collaboratively with organisations in six key communities:

- Cultural heritage organisations (including museums, national inventories, and archaeological organisations)
- Law-enforcement agencies
- Customs agencies
- The art trade
- Appraisers
- The insurance industry

The information needs of these organisations vary, but all need documentation that makes it possible to identify individual objects. Building a broad consensus across these communities on the categories of information essential for identifying objects was the essential precondition to a successful outcome for this initiative.

The first step toward establishing consensus on this core information was to identify and compare the information requirements of each of these communities, to understand the purposes for which their information is collected, and to determine how it is used and with whom it is shared. These requirements were identified by a combination of background research, interviews, and, most importantly, major international questionnaire surveys. The first of these surveys was carried out between July and December 1994 by the Getty Information Institute, with the endorsement of the Council of Europe, ICOM, and UNESCO. The survey elicited responses from organisations in 43 countries, including many major museums and galleries, heritage documentation centres, INTERPOL, and a number of national law-enforcement agencies. The survey also took account of existing standards and standards-making initiatives in the museum world, including those of the International Council of Museums, the Museum Documentation Association (UK), and the Canadian Heritage Information Network.

The results of this preliminary survey—published in July 1995 as *Protecting Cultural Objects through International Documentation Standards: A Preliminary Survey*—demonstrated that there did, indeed, exist a broad consensus on many of the categories of information that are candidates for inclusion in the proposed standard. Encouraged by these findings, the project went on to survey the information needs of the other key communities, namely dealers in art, antiques, and antiquities; appraisers of personal property; art insurance specialists; and customs agencies. Over 1,000 responses were received from organisations in 84 countries and dependencies, making this survey the largest of its kind ever carried out.

The findings of the questionnaire surveys were used to inform a series of roundtable meetings of experts drawn from the communities concerned. These began with a meeting of conservation specialists, held in Washington, D.C., in August 1994. This was the first meeting of an international Conservation Specialists Working Group organised jointly by the Getty Information Institute and the Getty Conservation Institute. A key recommendation of this meeting was that the standard should include a category called **Distinguishing Features**, the purpose of which would be to record information about an object's physical characteristics that could help to identify it (e.g., damage, repairs, or manufacturing defects).[10] The Washington roundtable was followed by a meeting of museum documentation experts, held in Edinburgh in November 1995. The standard recommended by the participants at this roundtable of experts has been little changed by the findings of subsequent surveys and the recommendations of later meetings. This gathering was an important milestone for the project in that it demonstrated the possibility of establishing a consensus among professionals within a key community. The third meeting was with art-insurance specialists, and was held at Lloyd's of London in March 1996. The fourth meeting—held at the Winterthur Museum in Delaware—brought together organisations representing dealers and appraisers of art, antiques, and antiquities. The final meeting, held in Prague in November 1996, was for representatives of law-enforcement agencies and commercial organisations that operate computerised art theft databases. It was organised in partnership with UNESCO and the Czech Ministry of Culture.

The findings of the surveys and recommendations of the roundtable meetings established that there was strong agreement on the categories of information that should constitute the standard (see *Protecting Cultural Objects in the Global Information Society: The Making of Object ID*, Getty Information Institute, 1997). The result is Object ID, a standard that is best defined in terms of the ways in which it can be implemented:

- It provides a checklist of the information required to identify stolen or missing objects,

- It is a documentation standard that establishes the minimum level of information needed to describe an object for purposes of identification,

- It is a key building block in the development of information networks that will allow divers organisations to exchange descriptions of objects rapidly,

- It provides a solid basis for training programmes that teach the documentation of objects.

The standard has been developed in response to an identified need, and is designed to be usable by non-specialists and to be capable of being implemented in traditional, non-computerised ways of making inventories and catalogues as well as in sophisticated computerised databases. Because Object ID is designed to be used by a number of communities, and by specialists and non-specialists alike, it identifies broad concepts rather than specific fields and uses simple, non-technical language. Similarly, its function as a checklist usable by the public led to the decision to present the definitions of the information categories in the form of questions—such as "What materials is the object made of?"—an approach that was found to be more comprehensible to non-specialists than definitions in the form of statements.

It is important to point out that Object ID is not an alternative to existing standards; rather it is a core standard created for a very specific purpose—that of describing cultural objects to enable them to be identified. As such it can be incorporated into existing systems and nested within existing standards. For example, in August 1997 the Executive Council of the International Council of Museums (ICOM) adopted a resolution that "A museum should be able to generate from its collection information system such data (preferably according to the 'Object ID' standard) that can identify an object in case of theft or looting." Similarly, it has been nested within the Spectrum standard for museum information developed by the Museum Documentation Association (UK). It has also been incorporated into a number of law-enforcement databases, including the National Stolen Art File of the Federal Bureau of Investigation (USA).

Combatting the illicit trade in cultural objects requires international collaboration among a variety of types of organisations in both the public and private sectors. The contribution of the Object ID project has been to identify a minimum standard for describing cultural objects, to encourage the making of descriptions of objects in both private and public ownership, and to bring together organisations that can encourage the implementation of the standard, as well as those that will play a part in developing networks along which this information can circulate.

# The Standards in Practice—
# The Example of Greenwich

*View of the Queen's House and Royal Naval College from Greenwich Park, London (copyright RCHME Crown Copyright).*

The Royal Naval College, the Queen's House, the Royal Observatory, and the Park at Greenwich constitute one of the most dramatic architectural and landscape ensembles in Europe, embodying a history that embraces royal patronage, maritime power, and scientific advance. The site includes evidence of settlement from the Roman period, a remarkable surviving group of Anglo-Saxon burial mounds, the remains of a 16th-century palace, a group of classical buildings designed by some of the greatest architects of the 17th and 18th centuries—Inigo Jones, Christopher Wren, and Nicholas Hawksmoor—and in the National Maritime Museum a remarkable collection that includes paintings, furniture, models, and historic timepieces. The principal buildings and landscape, and the nearby town centre, form part of the "Maritime Greenwich World Heritage Site," designated in December 1997. Moreover, in a publication about international standards it is fitting to use a location that gave its name to one of the earliest international agreements on the standardisation of practice—Greenwich Mean Time, established at the International Meridian Conference in Washington, D.C., in 1884.

For the purpose of illustrating the use of the core data standards, attention has been concentrated on the Royal Park, the multi-phase Queen's House to the north, and objects from the collections of the Museum that relate to the history of the site and to Greenwich's place in the history of the search for a method of establishing longitude at sea. Each of these sites and objects can be viewed and documented in isolation; equally, it is possible to show how they might be linked in a documentation system.

### Notes on Data Entry

*"Unique" and "Multiple Entry"*
In their recommendations for computer data entry, the Architectural and Archaeological Standards differ in their usage of "unique." In the Architectural Index, those categories for which a number of entries might be desired are designated "multiple entry"; those for which only one entry is required are designated "unique." In the Archaeological Standard, "multiple entry" is not used; "unique" is used to refer to a discrete item of information—different or multiple pieces of unique, discrete information may be contained within separate, repeating fields under one category heading.

*Cross Reference to Records of Fixtures and Fittings*
In the Architectural Index, cross references may be made to records of fixtures and fittings under Category 1.6. It is recommended that references to records of movable items related by location to the building are included in this category.

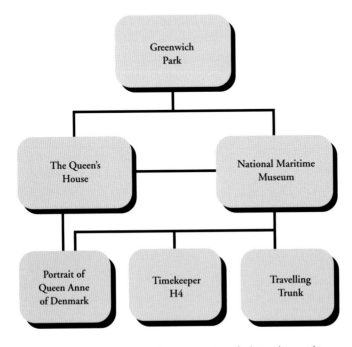

*Figure 3. Schematic representation of relationships within the Greenwich Ensemble*

**Sample Record 1:**

## Core Data Index to Historic Buildings and Monuments of the Architectural Heritage

*The Queen's House, Greenwich, was designed by Inigo Jones as a small private retreat for the Stuart Queens, Anne of Denmark and Henrietta Maria. Since the early nineteenth century the building has been in institutional use, first as part of the Royal Naval Asylum, amalgamated in 1821 with the Greenwich Hospital School, and now as the centrepiece of the National Maritime Museum. This sample record documents these three different uses: Domestic-House, Educational-School, Educational-Museum (see 3.0). Three principal construction phases are recorded: 1616–1619, 1629–1640 and 1661–1663 (see 4.0). Persons and organisations associated with the Queen's House are also recorded along with the roles they played in relation to the building, e.g.,: Inigo Jones (architect), Orazio Gentileschi (painter), Queen Anne of Denmark (patron), National Maritime Museum (occupier) and the dates at which these roles were played (see 5.0). The Queen's House forms part of the ensemble of the National Maritime Museum (1.5), and is linked to the archaeological record for Greenwich Park (1.8).*

| | | |
|---|---|---|
| 1.0 | Names and References | |
| 1.1 | Name of Building | **The Queen's House** |
| 1.2 | Reference Number | **610612** |
| 1.3 | Date of Compilation | **6th March 1998** |
| 1.4 | Recording Organisation | **Royal Commission on the Historical Monuments of England** |
| 1.5 | Cross Reference to Ensembles etc. | **National Maritime Museum** |
| 1.6 | Cross Reference to Fixtures and Movable Items | **[records of objects in National Maritime Museum]** |
| 1.7 | Cross Reference to Documentation | **TQ 3877 26/G53 (DoE List Reference)** |
| 1.8 | Cross Reference to Archaeology | **610514 [record for Greenwich Park]** |
| 1.9 | Cross Reference to Environment | |
| 2.0 | Location | |
| 2.1 | Administrative Location | |
| 2.1.1 | State | **United Kingdom** |
| 2.1.2 | Geo-political Unit | **England** |
| 2.1.3 | Sub-division | **London Borough of Greenwich** |
| 2.1.4 | Sub-division | |
| 2.2 | Address | |
| 2.2.1 | Postal Name | **National Maritime Museum** |

| | | | | | | |
|---|---|---|---|---|---|---|
| 2.2.2 | Number | | | | | |
| 2.2.3 | Street/Road | **Romney Road** | | | | |
| 2.2.4 | Locality | **Greenwich** | | | | |
| 2.2.5 | Town/City | **London** | | | | |
| 2.2.6 | Postal Code | **SE10 9NF** | | | | |
| 2.3 | Cartographic Reference | | | | | |
| 2.3.1 | X Coordinate | **5387** | | | | |
| 2.3.2 | Y Coordinate | **1777** | | | | |
| 2.3.3 | Spatial Referencing System | **Ordnance Survey** | | | | |
| 2.4 | Cadastral Reference/Land Unit | | | | | |
| 3.0 | Functional Type | | | | | |

| 3.1 | Type | 3.1.1 | Date | 3.2 | Category |
|---|---|---|---|---|---|
| | 1. **House** | | **1616–1807** | | **Domestic** |
| | 2. **School** | | **1807–1933** | | **Educational** |
| | 3. **Museum** | | **1937–** | | **Educational** |

| | | | |
|---|---|---|---|
| 4.0 | Dating | | |
| 4.1 | Period | | |
| 4.2 | Century | **17th century** | |
| 4.3 | Date Range | | |

| 4.3.1 | From | 4.3.2 | To |
|---|---|---|---|
| | 1. **1616** | | **1619** |
| | 2. **1629** | | **1640** |
| | 3. **1661** | | **1663** |

| | | |
|---|---|---|
| 4.4 | Absolute Date | |
| 5.0 | Persons & Organisations | |

| 5.1 | Name | 5.2 | Role | 5.2.1 | Date |
|---|---|---|---|---|---|
| | 1. **Jones, Inigo** | | **Architect** | | **1616–40** |
| | 2. **De Caus, Salomon** | | **Garden Designer** | | **1611–13** |
| | 3. **Gentileschi, Orazio** | | **Painter** | | **1636–38** |
| | 4. **Queen Anne of Denmark** | | **Patron** | | **1616–19** |
| | 5. **Queen Henrietta Maria** | | **Patron** | | **1629–40** |
| | 6. **Royal Naval Asylum/ Greenwich Hospital School** | | **Occupier** | | **1807–1933** |
| | 7. **National Maritime Museum** | | **Occupier** | | **1937–** |

6.0     Building Materials/Techniques

6.1     Walls

**Stone, Brick, Stucco**

6.2     Roof

**Leaded**

7.0     Physical Condition

7.1     General Condition

**Restored**

**Good**

8.0     Protection/Legal Status

| 8.1 Type | 8.2 Present Grade | 8.3 Date Granted |
|---|---|---|
| 1. **Listed Building** | **Grade I** | **8th June 1973** |
| 2. **Scheduled Ancient Monument** | — | **31st March 1994** |
| 3. **World Heritage Site** | — | **4th December 1997** |

9.0     Notes

9.1     Historical Summary

**The Queen's House was designed by Inigo Jones as a small private retreat for the Stuart Queens, Anne of Denmark and Henrietta Maria. Spanning the road which separated the Royal Palace from the Park at Greenwich, it was built in three phases between 1616 and 1663. The first truly classical Renaissance building to be erected in England, the house was sumptuously decorated and some of the finest art treasures of the Stuart Court were displayed there prior to the Civil War. Since the early nineteenth century the building has been in institutional use, first as part of the Royal Naval Asylum, amalgamated in 1821 with the Greenwich Hospital School, and now as the centrepiece of the National Maritime Museum. Restorations during the 1930s and 1980s have attempted to restore the building to its seventeenth-century appearance.**

**Sample Record 2:**

**Core Data Standard for Archaeological Sites and Monuments**

*Greenwich Park is a medieval deer park created in 1433. It subsequently became a royal park, associated with the Tudor palace of Placentia. The Park was redesigned in the 1660s as a formal landscape to accompany a proposed new royal palace following the Restoration of King Charles II. The site incorporates evidence of earlier settlement, including a Roman temple site and an Anglo-Saxon barrow cemetery. This record documents the medieval deer park of 1433, although it contains a cross reference to a record of the Anglo-Saxon Barrow cemetery (see 2.1.5.2).*

| | | |
|---|---|---|
| 2.1 | Name and References | |
| 2.1.1 | Reference Number | **610514** |
| 2.1.2 | Name of Monument or Site | **Greenwich Park** |
| 2.1.3 | Date of Compilation and Date of Last Update | |
| 2.1.3.1 | Date of Compilation | **1998-01-25** |
| 2.1.3.2 | Date of Last Update | **1998-03-13** |
| 2.1.4 | Originator of Reference | **Royal Commission on the Historical Monuments of England** |
| 2.1.5 | Cross Reference to Related Records of Monuments or Sites | |
| 2.1.5.1 | Reference Number | **404328; 610612** |
| 2.1.5.2 | Qualifier of Relationship | **Contains Anglo-Saxon Barrows; Related to the Queen's House** |
| 2.1.5.3 | Originator of Reference | **Royal Commission on the Historical Monuments of England** |
| 2.1.6 | Cross Reference to Archaeological Collections and Artefacts | |
| 2.1.7 | Cross Reference to Documentation | |
| 2.1.7.1 | Reference Number | **910061** |
| 2.1.7.2 | Type of Documentation/Archive | **Unpublished Text, Graphic, Photographic** |
| 2.1.7.3 | Originator of Reference | **Royal Commission on the Historical Monuments of England** |
| 2.1.8 | Cross Reference to Archaeological Events | |
| 2.1.8.1 | Reference Number | **1012515** |
| 2.1.8.2 | Type of Event | **Survey** |
| 2.1.8.3 | Start Date of Recording Event | **1993-09** |

| | | |
|---|---|---|
| 2.1.8.4 | End Date of Recording Event | **1994-02** |
| 2.1.8.5 | Originator of Reference | **Royal Commission on the Historical Monuments of England** |
| 2.2 | Location | |
| 2.2.1 | Administrative Location | |
| 2.2.1.1 | Country or Nation | **United Kingdom** |
| 2.2.1.2 | Geo-political Unit | **England** |
| 2.2.1.3 | Administrative Sub-division | **London Borough of Greenwich** |
| 2.2.2 | Site Location | |
| 2.2.2.1 | Description of Location | **On the south bank of the River Thames, seven miles south-east of central London** |
| 2.2.3 | Address | |
| 2.2.3.1 | Name for Address Purposes | **Greenwich Park** |
| 2.2.3.2 | Number in the Street/Road | |
| 2.2.3.3 | Name of Street/Road | |
| 2.2.3.4 | Locality | **Greenwich** |
| 2.2.3.5 | Town or City | **London** |
| 2.2.3.6 | Postal Code | **SE10 8QY** |
| 2.2.4 | Cadastral Reference/Land Unit | |
| 2.2.5 | Cartographic Reference | |
| 2.2.5.1 | Cartographic Identifier | |
| 2.2.5.2 | Spatial Referencing System | **Ordnance Survey** |
| 2.2.5.3 | Topology | **P [point]** |
| 2.2.5.4 | Qualifier | **Centre** |
| 2.2.5.5 | Sequence Number | |
| 2.2.5.6 | Z Coordinate | |
| 2.2.5.7 | X Coordinate | **5390** |
| 2.2.5.8 | Y Coordinate | **1770** |
| 2.3 | Type | |
| 2.3.1 | Monument or Site Type | **Deer Park** |
| 2.3.2 | Monument or Site Category | **Gardens, Parks and Urban Spaces** |
| 2.4 | Dating | |
| 2.4.1 | Cultural Period | |
| 2.4.1.1 | Cultural Period | **Medieval** |
| 2.4.2 | Century | |

| 2.4.2.1 | Century | **15th century** | |
|---------|---------|-----------------|---|
| 2.4.3 | Date Range | | |
| 2.4.3.1 | From Date | **1433** | |
| 2.4.3.2 | To Date | **1540** | |
| 2.4.4 | Scientific and Absolute Dates | | |
| 2.4.4.1 | Date | | |
| 2.4.4.2 | Method | | |
| 2.5 | Physical Condition | | |
| 2.5.1 | Condition | **Intact** | |
| 2.5.2 | Date Condition Assessed | **1994-02** | |
| 2.6 | Designation/Protection Status | | |

| 2.6.1 | Type of Designation or Protection | 2.6.2 | Date of Designation or Protection |
|-------|-----------------------------------|-------|-----------------------------------|
| | 1. **Register of Parks and Gardens—Grade I** | | **January 1988** |
| | 2. **World Heritage Site** | | **4th December 1997** |
| 2.6.3 | Reference Number | 2.6.4 | Originator of Reference |
| | 1. — | | **English Heritage** |
| | 2. — | | **UNESCO** |

| 2.7 | Archaeological Summary | |
|-----|------------------------|---|

**Greenwich Park is a medieval deer park created by Duke Humphrey of Gloucester in 1433 to complement his residence on the south bank of the River Thames. It subsequently became a royal park, associated with the Tudor palace of Placentia. It incorporates evidence of earlier settlement, including a Roman temple site and an Anglo-Saxon barrow cemetery. The Park was redesigned in the 1660s as a formal landscape to the south of the Queen's House, to accompany a proposed new royal palace following the Restoration of King Charles II. It now has the character of an urban, public park.**

**Sample Record 3:**

# Object ID

*Portrait of Queen Anne of Denmark, attributed to John de Critz, the elder (copyright National Maritime Museum, Greenwich, London).*

| | | |
|---|---|---|
| 1.1 | Photographs | **National Maritime Museum - BHC 4251** |
| 1.2 | Type of Object | |
| | *Level 1:* | **Painting** |
| | *Level 2:* | **Portrait** |
| 1.3 | Measurements | **114 x 87 cm** |
| 1.4 | Materials & Techniques | **Oil on panel** |
| 1.5 | Inscriptions & Markings | **Christie's stencil on back "NV336," and another which appears to read "ENDOPH1"** |
| 1.6 | Date or Period | **c. 1605** |
| 1.7 | Maker | **Attributed to John de Critz, the elder** |
| 1.8 | Subject | **Queen Anne of Denmark / Woman in white dress holding fan** |
| 1.9 | Title | **Portrait of Queen Anne of Denmark** |

| 1.10 | Distinguishing Features | **Damaged by criss-cross scoring on the lower part of the dress. The oak panel is in three sections, shaved down to 1/4-inch thickness, subsequently cradled on the back. There is old woodworm damage and two new flight holes. The carved and gilded frame appears to be 17th century Italian. There are traces of green paint on the tooled Spanish leather background.** |
|---|---|---|
| 1.11 | Description | **A three-quarter-length portrait of Queen Anne of Denmark, the wife of King James I, at the age of about 30. The Queen is dressed in a white farthingale, with piled-up hair, adorned with a jewel and a pearl. She is wearing pearls around her neck and her bodice, and is holding a fan in her left hand. There is a chair in the background. An almost identical portrait exists at Blickling Hall, Norfolk, on which there has been over-painting at an early date, bringing the hairstyle and ruff into a style which she assumed in or before 1609.** |

| 2.1 | Object ID No. | **National Maritime Museum - BHC 4251** |
|---|---|---|
| 2.2 | Related Written Material | **NMM, *The Maritime Yearbook*, 3, 1995/96, 11–13; National Maritime Museum dossier and conservation record.** |
| 2.3 | Place of Origin/Discovery | **England** |
| 2.4 | Cross Reference to Related Objects | **There is likely to have been a pendant portrait of James I, but its whereabouts are unknown.** |
| 2.5 | Date Documented | **16th March 1998** |

**Sample Record 4:**

# Object ID

*Travelling Trunk (copyright National Maritime Museum, Greenwich, London).*

| | | |
|---|---|---|
| 1.1 | Photographs | **National Maritime Museum - A 1891, A 1892** |
| 1.2 | Type of Object | |
| | *Level 1:* | **Furniture** |
| | *Level 2:* | **Travelling trunk** |
| 1.3 | Measurements | **81 cm high x 67 cm deep x 120 cm long** |
| 1.4 | Materials & Techniques | **Wood, leather-covered and brass-studded, canvas-lined** |
| 1.5 | Inscriptions & Markings | **Date and initials in brass studs in the centre of the lid "G 1660 P"** |
| 1.6 | Date or Period | **1660** |
| 1.7 | Maker | |
| 1.8 | Subject | |
| 1.9 | Title | |
| 1.10 | Distinguishing Features | **The handles are missing and the inside modernised; there is splitting and lifting of the leather covering at the edges of the lid.** |

| 1.11 | Description | An early travelling trunk, possibly owned by George Parnall (GP), who was Mayor of Hereford in 1660. Leather-covered and brass-studded, with a curved lid which fits over flanges. Inside, there is a lift-out wooden tray resting on yellow pine bearers. Both the tray and the canvas lining were added at a later date. A similar trunk with the royal cypher and crown, given by Queen Henrietta Maria to Lord St Albans, was at Rushbrooke Hall, Bury St Edmunds, Suffolk. |

---

| 2.1 | Object ID Number | **National Maritime Museum - AAA 3250** |
| 2.2 | Related Written Material | **NMM Furniture file** |
| 2.3 | Place of Origin/Discovery | **England** |
| 2.4 | Cross Reference to Related Objects | |
| 2.5 | Date Documented | **16th March 1998** |

**Sample Record 5:**

# Object ID

*John Harrison's marine timekeeper, H4 (copyright National Maritime Museum, Greenwich, London).*

| | | |
|---|---|---|
| 1.1 | Photographs | **National Maritime Museum - A 6269** |
| 1.2 | Type of Object | |
| | *Level 1:* | **Timekeeper** |
| | *Level 2:* | **Chronometer** |
| 1.3 | Measurements | **13.2 cm diameter, 5.5 cm deep; 1.45 kg weight** |
| 1.4 | Materials & Techniques | **Silver, brass and steel; glass; enamel on copper dial; diamonds and rubies in the bearings; silk lining to the case.** |
| 1.5 | Inscriptions & Markings | **Signed "John Harrison and Son, London AD 1759" on the movement; silver hallmarks on the outer (dated 1759) and inner (dated 1758) cases; makers' marks on the outer ("HT") and inner ("IH") cases.** |

| 1.6 | Date or Period | **1759** |
|---|---|---|
| 1.7 | Maker | **John Harrison and Son, London** |
| 1.8 | Subject | |
| 1.9 | Title | **Marine timekeeper, H4** |
| 1.10 | Distinguishing Features | **There is a crack in the enamel of the dial and a triangular chip in the enamel near the case bolt.** |
| 1.11 | Description | **A marine timekeeper in the form of a silver pair-cased watch, with a brass and steel fusee movement with Harrison's verge escapement with diamond pallets. The watch represents the successful conclusion to Harrison's work in developing a high-accuracy, portable, marine timekeeper, enabling the establishment of longitude at sea. It is the first precision watch.** |

| 2.1 | Object ID Number | **National Maritime Museum - ZAA 0037** |
|---|---|---|
| 2.2 | Related Written Material | **NMM departmental file; J. Betts, *Harrison*, London, 1993; R.T. Gould, *The Marine Chronometer—Its History and Development*, London, 1923; H. Quill, *John Harrison, the Man Who Found Longitude*, London, 1966.** |
| 2.3 | Place of Origin/Discovery | **England** |
| 2.4 | Cross Reference to Related Objects | **This is one in a sequence of 5 prototypes of which H4 was the successful conclusion and H5 was a similar model, based on H4. H1, 2 and 3 are in the National Maritime Museum; H5 is at the Worshipful Company of Clockmakers, Guildhall, London.** |
| 2.5 | Date Documented | **25th March 1998** |

# Core Data Index to Historic Buildings and Monuments of the Architectural Heritage

## Definitions

The following presents the definitions of the headings proposed for the Core Data Index. Headings 1 to 4 are mandatory:

1. Names and References
2. Location
3. Functional Type
4. Dating

The others, 5 to 9, are optional and will vary according to the nature of the record held and to the individual organisational requirements:

**1.0    Names and References**

**1.1    Name of Building**

A free-text field which records the name by which a building is known. Not intended as a retrieval term, it may be used in conjunction with the searchable fields — Location (2.1), Address (2.2), Functional Type (3.1).
*(Alphanumeric, Free Text, Multiple Entry, Optional)*

**1.2    Unique Reference Number**

The number or combination of characters which uniquely identifies each building recorded by the organisation.
*(Alphanumeric, Unique, Mandatory)*

**1.3    Date of Compilation**

Date of compilation of the core data index record. This date may be modified whenever the index record is updated.
*(Alphanumeric, Unique, Mandatory)*

**1.4    Recording Organisation**

Name of the organisation responsible for curating the record. This information is useful in establishing the provenance of the record when data is exchanged between recording organisations.
*(Alphanumeric, Unique, Mandatory)*

**1.5**    **Cross Reference to Related Building Records**
This enables cross referencing to related records, enabling, for example, the relating of a building record to its wider complex record.
*(Alphanumeric, Multiple Entry, Optional)*

**1.5.1**   **Qualifier of Relationship**
This field indicates the type of relationship between one recorded structure and another, such as a hierarchical "parent–child" relationship linking a building complex (e.g., Monastery) and an individual building (e.g., Church).
*(Alphanumeric, Multiple Entry, Optional)*

**1.6**    **Cross Reference to Records of Fixtures and Fittings**
This enables cross referencing to related records of stained glass, wall paintings, sculptural decoration, etc., which relate to the building.
*(Alphanumeric, Multiple Entry, Optional)*

**1.7**    **Cross Reference to Documentation**
This enables cross referencing to the documentation associated with the indexed record and may be separable as follows:

**1.7.1**   **Photographic Reference Number(s)**
*(Alphanumeric, Multiple Entry, Optional)*

**1.7.2**   **Graphic Reference Number(s)**
*(Alphanumeric, Multiple Entry, Optional)*

**1.7.3**   **Textual Sources Reference Number(s)**
*(Alphanumeric, Multiple Entry, Optional)*

**1.7.4**   **Bibliographic Reference Number(s)**
*(Alphanumeric, Multiple Entry, Optional)*

**1.8**    **Cross Reference to Archaeological Records**
To relate, for example, records of archaeological excavations to those of standing structures on the same site.
*(Alphanumeric, Multiple Entry, Optional)*

**1.9**    **Cross Reference to Environmental Records**
To enable the association of the building record with other records which may detail levels of environmental protection relevant to the site or locality.
*(Alphanumeric, Multiple Entry, Optional)*

**2.0**    **Location**
A combination of the fields defined in the sections below may be employed to identify the location of the building.

## 2.1   Administrative Location

### 2.1.1   State
*(Alphanumeric, Unique, Mandatory for Data Exchange)*

### 2.1.2   Geo-political Unit
Used for recording geographical or political subdivisions of member states.
*(Alphanumeric, Unique, Optional)*

### 2.1.3   State Administrative Division(s)
According to the administrative structure of each member state, a number of repeat entries for this field may be required.
*(Alphanumeric, Multiple Entry, Optional)*

### 2.1.4   Administrative Sub-division
*(Alphanumeric, Multiple Entry, Optional)*
According to the administrative structure of each member state, more sub-divisions may be required.

## 2.2   Address

### 2.2.1   Postal Name
Use this field if the name differs from 1.1.
*(Alphanumeric, Unique, Optional)*

### 2.2.2   Number in the Street/Road
*(Alphanumeric, Unique, Optional)*

### 2.2.3   Name of Street/Road
*(Alphanumeric, Unique, Optional)*

### 2.2.4   Locality
Used for commonly known non-administrative units such as hamlets and townships.
*(Alphanumeric, Unique, Optional)*

### 2.2.5   Town/City
Use this field if the name differs from the State Administrative Division.
*(Alphanumeric, Unique, Optional)*

### 2.2.6   Postal Code
*(Alphanumeric, Unique, Optional)*

**2.3** **Cartographic Reference**
These fields are used to record the two-dimensional Cartesian, spatial co-ordinates required for locating the building against the mapping system(s) used by member states.

**2.3.1** **X Coordinates**
*(Numeric, Multiple Entry, Optional)*

**2.3.2** **Y Coordinates**
*(Numeric, Multiple Entry, Optional)*

**2.3.3** **Spatial Referencing System Employed**
e.g., UTM, Lambert, UPS, Ordnance Survey
*(Alphanumeric, Unique, Optional)*

**2.4** **Cadastral Reference/Land Unit**
Enables cross reference to the land unit/parcel(s) current in some member states.
*(Alphanumeric, Multiple Entry, Optional)*

**3.0** **Functional Type**

**3.1** **Building Type**
Precise building type defined by function. This field may be repeated to accommodate changes in type over a period of time. Controlled vocabulary is desirable.
*(Alphanumeric, Multiple Entry, Mandatory)*

**3.1.1** **Date**
The date to which the specific function in 3.1 is assigned.
*(Alphanumeric, Multiple Entry, Optional)*

**3.2** **Building Category**
Broad functional category to which the building type belongs, e.g., Agricultural (Category); Barn (Type). Controlled vocabulary is desirable.
*(Alphanumeric, Multiple Entry, Mandatory)*

**4.0** **Dating**
This section allows for precise dating when it is known, or date ranges or periods when it is imprecise.
*(One field at least is mandatory)*

**4.1** **Period**
Controlled vocabulary is desirable. e.g., Paleolithic
*(Alphanumeric, Multiple Entry, Optional)*

**4.2** **Century**
e.g., 17th century
*(Alphanumeric, Multiple Entry, Optional)*

**4.3** **Date Range**

**4.3.1** **From**

**4.3.2** **To**
e.g., from 1640 to 1660
*(Numeric, Multiple Entry, Optional)*

**4.4** **Absolute Date**
e.g., 1652
*(Numeric, Multiple Entry, Optional)*

**5.0** **Persons and Organisations Associated with the History of the Building**
This section allows for the identification of persons and organisations associated either with the construction of the building, e.g., architects, or its function, e.g., the original proprietors. The fields may be repeated to accommodate persons and organisations associated with the buildings over a period of time. Detailed information may be held in related biographical files.

**5.1** **Person or Organisation**
Surname, first name, or name of organisation, e.g., Webb, John
*(Alphanumeric, Multiple Entry, Optional)*

**5.2** **Role in the History of the Building**
The role of the person or organisation with respect to the building, i.e., its construction, function, restoration, modification, demolition, etc., e.g., architect.
*(Alphanumeric, Multiple Entry, Optional)*

**5.2.1** **Date**
The date of the person or organisation's role in the history of the building, e.g., 1652.
*(Numeric, Multiple Entry, Optional)*

**6.0** **Building Materials and Techniques**

**6.1    Main Materials and Structural Techniques**
This field should be used for the main walling material, excluding partition walls. A controlled vocabulary is desirable.
*(Alphanumeric, Multiple Entry, Optional)*

**6.2    Covering Materials**
The main roofing material. A controlled vocabulary is desirable.
*(Alphanumeric, Multiple Entry, Optional)*

**7.0    Physical Condition**

**7.1    General Condition**
This field may be repeated in order to distinguish between the integrity of the building (demolished, ruined, remodelled, restored) and its state (good, fair, poor, or bad). A controlled vocabulary is desirable.
*(Alphanumeric, Multiple Entry, Optional)*

**8.0    Protection/Legal Status**
This section allows for statements on whether the building is protected and, if so, the type of protection and the date at which it was granted.

**8.1    Type of Protection**
*(Alphanumeric, Multiple Entry, Optional)*

**8.2    Grade of Protection**
*(Alphanumeric, Multiple Entry, Optional)*

**8.3    Date at which Protection was Granted**
*(Alphanumeric, Multiple Entry, Optional)*

**9.0    Notes**

**9.1    Historical Summary**
This optional field allows for a brief textual summary of the historical development of the building, which is particularly useful if information for sections 3–5 above cannot be identified precisely.

# International
## Core Data Standard for
## Archaeological Sites
## and Monuments

**1.0**    **Using the Core Data Standard**

The various sections into which the data standard is divided represent the minimum categories of information required to make a reasonable assessment of a monument or site, whether for planning, management, academic, or other purposes. In addition, reference can be provided to further information held in databases, document centres, and elsewhere which may be necessary for the detailed understanding and care of individual monuments or sites or categories of monument or site.

The mandatory sections within the data standard provide for a minimum amount of information required for indexing in structured fields and describing in free-text fields an archaeological monument or site. The optional sections, sub-sections, and fields allow for the recording of a monument or site in greater detail. For example, a site may be cross referenced to a larger complex of which it forms a part, or to records of excavations undertaken on the site. Cross referencing can also be made to more detailed documentary information either held by or known to the organisation responsible for the particular monument or site record. Clearly the level of recording undertaken by individual organisations will vary according to its own requirements and resources.

Not all the sections are mandatory. Each section contains a varying number of sub-sections, some of which are mandatory (i.e., the information must be recorded), while others are optional (i.e., recording of information depends upon the priorities of the recording organisation). Alternatively, of course, the information may not exist. For example, there may never have been an excavation undertaken at a particular site, in which case sub-section 2.1.8 cannot be completed.

While many of the sub-sections are optional, once it has been decided to record the type of information they refer to, then some or all of the fields within the sub-sections become mandatory. For example, if it is decided to make cross reference to records of archaeological excavations/events (sub-section 2.1.8), then the reference number of that excavation record and the name of the organisation responsible for curating that record must be entered.

The individual sections are as follows:

- Section 2.1 identifies the monument or site, and allows cross referencing to records of events, e.g., excavation and/or survey undertaken at that site, and to records of artefactual and archival material associated with the site.

- Section 2.2 locates the monument or site in terms of address, political, cartographic, and other spatial criteria.

- Section 2.3 describes the type of monument or site being recorded.

- Section 2.4 allows for a date to be assigned to a monument or site, or for dates to be assigned to particular phases of use.

- Section 2.5 records the physical condition of the monument or site.

- Section 2.6 permits a note to be made of any form of protection, legislative or otherwise, which applies to the monument or site.

- Section 2.7 provides for a brief summary of what is known, archaeologically, about the monument or site.

Although many of the entry fields within the sections and sub-sections require only a single piece of information (designated "unique" within the data standard), it is recognised that in certain instances two or more terms may be relevant to a particular monument or site within a single field, sub-section, or section. For example, an archaeological site may straddle the border of two adjacent administrative areas, or more than one excavation may have taken place at a particular site. In such instances, the data standard recommends the repetition of the whole sub-section or section rather than multiple entry, within one field. Thus in the example of more than one excavation at a particular site, each would be treated as a separate event, and the whole of the cross references in 2.1.8 would be repeated for each excavation record.

**Implementation of the Core Data Standard**

The core data standard presented here has been devised within a theoretical framework which can be employed in both manual and computer-based systems. Organisations proposing to implement the data standard are likely to build on the data standard and its theoretical framework to meet their own recording needs. The standard prepared by CIDOC draws much from the practical experience of organisations that have already implemented heritage databases, e.g., DKC, Denmark; MONARCH, England; DRACAR, France; and ARCHIS, the Netherlands.

An important element of the data standard, and of archaeological databases, is the means by which the various sections are linked. The relationship between different categories of information is as important as those individual categories of information themselves. Thus within any database implementing the data standard presented here, all sections would need to be connected to section 2.1, which identifies the monument or site, names the source of the record, and provides the date on which the record was compiled. However, in addition, other sections need to be closely linked to each other. For example, there is a clear need for a particularly close relationship to be established between section 2.3 (Type) and section 2.4 (Dating) in order to allow explicit links to be made between monument or site type and period for multi-period monuments or sites whose character changed through time, e.g., Enclosed Settlement/Bronze Age; Open Settlement/Iron Age; Villa/Roman.

**2.0    The Core Data Standard**

The following presents the definitions of the sections, sub-sections, and fields contained within the Core Data Standard. Some of these are mandatory. Others are optional, and the need to complete them will vary according to the nature of the record held and to the individual organisational requirements.

**2.1    Names and References**

This is a mandatory section which identifies the monument or site.

**2.1.1    Reference Number**

The number or combination of characters which uniquely identifies each monument or site recorded by the organisation within its database, e.g., 615649. *(Alphanumeric, Unique, Mandatory)*

**2.1.2    Name of Monument or Site**

A free-text field which records the name or names by which a monument or site was or is known, e.g., Stonehenge. *(Alphanumeric, Unique, Optional)*

**2.1.3    Date of Compilation and Date of Last Update**

This sub-section records the date of compilation of the site or monument record, and the date on which that record was last amended.

**2.1.3.1    Date of Compilation**

The date on which the core record was created. Use of the ISO standard for date is recommended, e.g., 1986-06-22. *(Alphanumeric, Unique, Mandatory)*

**2.1.3.2    Date of Last Update**

The date on which the monument or site record was last added to, altered, or amended. Use of the ISO standard for date is recommended, e.g., 1993-07-12. *(Alphanumeric, Unique, Mandatory)*

### 2.1.4 Originator of Reference

The name of the individual or organisation responsible for curating the monument or site record. This information is useful in establishing the provenance of the record when data is exchanged between recording organisations, e.g., RCAHMW.
*(Alphanumeric, Unique, Mandatory)*

### 2.1.5 Cross Reference to Related Records of Monuments or Sites

This sub-section enables cross referencing to records of related monuments or sites. For example, relating a record to its wider complex record, e.g., a house within a settlement. It is optional and can be repeated.

### 2.1.5.1 Reference Number

The number or combination of characters which uniquely identifies each related record, e.g., SM97342.
*(Alphanumeric, Unique, Mandatory)*

### 2.1.5.2 Qualifier of Relationship

The qualifier indicates the type of relationship between one record and another, such as a hierarchical "parent–child" relationship linking an archaeological complex and an individual site. The entry will be one of the following: "Part of," "Contains," or "Related to." In the example of a record for a house, the relationship to a settlement would be "Part of." In the record for the settlement, the relationship to the house would be "Contains." The house could also have a relationship of "Related to" another house within the same settlement.
*(Alphanumeric, Unique, Mandatory)*

### 2.1.5.3 Originator of Reference

The name of the individual or organisation responsible for curating the related record, e.g., Ministry of Culture.
*(Alphanumeric, Unique, Mandatory)*

### 2.1.6 Cross Reference to Archaeological Collections and Artefacts

This sub-section enables cross referencing to related records of archaeological collections. It is optional and can be repeated.

### 2.1.6.1 Reference Number

The number or combination of characters which uniquely identifies each related collection or artefact record, e.g., 57486.
*(Alphanumeric, Unique, Mandatory)*

### 2.1.6.2 Originator of Reference

The name of the individual or organisation responsible for curating the related record, e.g., Nationalmuseet (DKC).
*(Alphanumeric, Unique, Mandatory)*

### 2.1.7 Cross Reference to Documentation

This sub-section enables cross referencing to the published and unpublished documentation associated with the site or monument. It is optional and can be repeated.

#### 2.1.7.1 Reference Number

The number or combination of characters which uniquely identifies each related piece of documentation, e.g., DD27483.
*(Alphanumeric, Unique, Mandatory)*

#### 2.1.7.2 Type of Documentation/Archive

The type of documentation or archive associated with the site. Controlled vocabulary is desirable, e.g., photographic, graphic, unpublished text, bibliographic, electronic, cartographic.
*(Alphanumeric, Unique, Mandatory)*

#### 2.1.7.3 Originator of Reference

The name of the individual or organisation responsible for curating the related documentation record, e.g., Royal Commission on the Historical Monuments of England.
*(Alphanumeric, Unique, Mandatory)*

### 2.1.8 Cross Reference to Archaeological Events

This sub-section makes it possible to relate, for example, records of archaeological excavations or surveys to those of the monument or site. Where multiple events have occurred at a monument or site (e.g., a survey followed by excavation) separate entries in this sub-section should be completed. It is an optional sub-section which can be repeated.

#### 2.1.8.1 Reference Number

The number or combination of characters which uniquely identifies each related event record, e.g., CX974\38.
*(Alphanumeric, Unique, Mandatory)*

#### 2.1.8.2 Type of Event

The nature of the event, e.g., excavation, survey. Where multiple events have occurred, each should have a separate entry.
*(Alphanumeric, Unique, Mandatory)*

#### 2.1.8.3 Start Date of Recording Event

The date on which the recording event commenced. Use of the ISO standard for date is recommended, e.g., 1896-07-03.
*(Alphanumeric, Unique, Optional)*

**2.1.8.4  End Date of Recording Event**

The date on which the recording event terminated.  Use of the ISO standard for date is recommended, e.g., 1896-07-30.
*(Alphanumeric, Unique, Optional)*

**2.1.8.5  Originator of Reference**

The name of the individual or organisation responsible for curating the related event record, e.g., Department of Environmental Affairs and Tourism.
*(Alphanumeric, Unique, Optional)*

**2.2  Location**

This is a mandatory section which defines the spatial location of the monument or site in terms of political, postal, geographic, and cartographic criteria.

Any combination of sub-sections defined below may be employed to identify the location of the monument or site.  More than one type of sub-section may be used to more closely determine the location or to make otherwise ambiguous locations more precise.  It should be noted that at least one sub-section must be used but that no individual sub-section is mandatory.

**2.2.1  Administrative Location**

This is an optional sub-section for details of administrative location.  It can be repeated.

**2.2.1.1  Country or Nation**

The name of the country or nation within which the monument or site is located, e.g., France.
*(Alphanumeric, Unique, Optional (Mandatory for exchanging data with other countries))*

**2.2.1.2  Geo-political Unit**

This is used for recording the geographical or political subdivisions of countries or nations within which the monument or site is located; for instance Regions in France, Lander in Germany, Counties in Great Britain.
*(Alphanumeric, Unique, Mandatory)*

**2.2.1.3  Administrative Sub-division**

This is used for recording the further administrative sub-divisions appropriate to the monument or site.  According to the administrative structure of each nation or country, a number of repeat entries in this field may be required.  For example, in Great Britain the Country, England, is further subdivided into County, District and Parish, e.g., Wiltshire, Salisbury, Amesbury, and so would require three entries.
*(Alphanumeric, Unique, Mandatory)*

It should be noted that it is essential to differentiate between the different levels of administrative sub-divisions which relate to each site or monument, e.g., local or regional.

### 2.2.2 Site Location

This is an optional sub-section which provides for a free-text explanation of the location of the site or monument.

### 2.2.2.1 Description of Location

A free-text field enabling a short description of the location of a monument or site to be recorded, to assist identification in the field, and to provide a more precise location for sites in sparsely populated or poorly mapped areas.
*(Alphanumeric, Unique, Mandatory)*

### 2.2.3 Address

This enables the recording of the location of monuments or sites which have a postal address, especially those within built-up areas. It is an optional sub-section and can be repeated. For example, if the monument or site is located on two streets or has two postal names. All the fields are optional, but at least one must be completed.

### 2.2.3.1 Name for Address Purposes

Use this field to record the name of the monument or site for address purposes (or postal name), e.g., Cruive Cottage.
*(Alphanumeric, Unique, Optional)*

### 2.2.3.2 Number in the Street or Road

Use this field for the number of the monument or site in the street or road, e.g., 27A.
*(Alphanumeric, Unique, Optional)*

### 2.2.3.3 Name of Street or Road

Use this field for the name of the street or road, e.g., Calea Victoriei.
*(Alphanumeric, Unique, Optional)*

### 2.2.3.4 Locality

Use this field for commonly known non-administrative units such as hamlets and townships, e.g., Pincevent.
*(Alphanumeric, Unique, Optional)*

### 2.2.3.5 Town or City

Use this field for the name of the town or city, e.g., Stockholm.
*(Alphanumeric, Unique, Optional)*

### 2.2.3.6 Postal or Other Similar National Address Code
Use this field to record an address code, e.g., 670000, K1A OC8
*(Alphanumeric, Unique, Optional)*

### 2.2.4 Cadastral Reference/Land Unit
Some countries operate a system of allocating reference numbers to individual blocks or units of land. The land unit reference number relevant to the particular monument or site can be entered here. This field is optional and can be repeated.

### 2.2.4.1 Cadastral Reference
This field enables cross reference to the land unit or parcel(s) current in some nations or countries, e.g., block reference 941\278.
*(Alphanumeric, Unique, Mandatory)*

### 2.2.5 Cartographic Reference
This is an optional sub-section used to record the two- or three-dimensional or spatial co-ordinates required for locating the monument or site within the mapping system(s) used by individual countries or nations. The four fields 2.2.5.5–8 should be repeated for each set of co-ordinates.

### 2.2.5.1 Cartographic Identifier
The identifier of the cartographic entity where the monument or site has more than one such entity related to it, e.g., polygon 1.
*(Alphanumeric, Unique, Optional)*

### 2.2.5.2 Spatial Referencing System
This field specifies the spatial or cartographic referencing system employed, e.g., UTM, Lambert, GPS, Ordnance Survey.
*(Alphanumeric, Unique, Mandatory)*

### 2.2.5.3 Topology
This field specifies whether the spatial co-ordinates given relate to a point, line, or area, e.g., P, L, A.
*(Alphanumeric, Unique, Mandatory)*

### 2.2.5.4 Qualifier
This field allows for an indication of the significance and reliability of the cartographic or spatial co-ordinates for a site or monument, e.g., approximate, centre. Controlled vocabulary is desirable.
*(Alphanumeric, Unique, Mandatory)*

The following four fields should be repeated for each co-ordinate.

### 2.2.5.5  Sequence Number

When an archaeological site or monument is of linear or polygonal shape, it is advisable to list a series of sets of co-ordinates describing its course rather than a single reference to, for example, its central point. These should be listed in sequence. The sequence number for each set of co-ordinates should be entered here. For example, 1 for a point, 1,2 for a line and 1,2,3 for a polygon.
*(Alphanumeric, Unique, Mandatory)*

### 2.2.5.6  Z Coordinate

Value or identifier of cartographic reference. It locates a record in relation to a vertical datum, e.g., 30 metres above sea-level, 30 metres below chart datum for underwater sites.
*(Alphanumeric, Unique, Optional)*

### 2.2.5.7  X Coordinate

Value or identifier of cartographic reference. This is normally the east–west coordinate.
*(Numeric, Unique, Mandatory)*

### 2.2.5.8  Y Coordinate

Value or identifier of cartographic reference. This is normally the north–south coordinate.
*(Numeric, Unique, Mandatory)*

### 2.3  Type

This section allows for the indexing of a monument or site according to functional or descriptive criteria. An entry is mandatory and must be linked to an entry in section 2.4 (Dating), e.g., Villa/Roman. Controlled vocabulary is necessary and should include "unknown." This section can be repeated to accommodate changes in a type at a monument or site through time.

### 2.3.1  Monument or Site Type

The term by which a monument has been indexed. This will normally be the interpretation of the monument by functional or descriptive criteria, e.g., Villa; linear earthwork. Controlled vocabulary is desirable.
*(Alphanumeric, Unique, Mandatory)*

### 2.3.2  Monument or Site Category

Broad functional or descriptive category to which the type belongs, e.g., Residential. Controlled vocabulary is desirable. Note that if a hierarchical thesaurus is being used this field may not be required.
*(Alphanumeric, Unique, Optional)*

### 2.4 Dating

This is a mandatory section allowing for the recording of precise dating when it is known, or date ranges or periods when it is imprecise. This section can be repeated. An entry in this section should be linked to one in section 2.3.

Sub-section 2.4.1 is mandatory, but one or more of the optional sub-sections which follow it may be employed to define the dating more closely.

### 2.4.1 Cultural Period

This is a mandatory sub-section allowing for the indexing of a site or monument according to the cultural period to which it has been assigned.

### 2.4.1.1 Cultural Period

The cultural period to which the monument or site, or a part or phase of the monument or site, belongs: e.g., Neolithic. A controlled vocabulary is desirable and must include "unknown."
*(Alphanumeric, Unique, Mandatory)*

### 2.4.2 Century

This is an optional sub-section for recording the century to which the site or monument, or a part of it, belongs.

### 2.4.2.1 Century

The century of the monument or site, e.g., 17th century. This field is only appropriate for monuments or sites which belong to historic periods.
*(Alphanumeric, Unique, Mandatory)*

### 2.4.3 Date Range

This is an optional sub-section for recording the date range which encompasses the use of the monument or site, or a particular phase of activity at the monument or site.

### 2.4.3.1 From Date

The earliest date in the range, e.g., 1640.
*(Alphanumeric, Unique, Mandatory)*

### 2.4.3.2 To Date

The latest date in the range, e.g., 1660.
*(Alphanumeric, Unique, Mandatory)*

### 2.4.4 Scientific and Absolute Dates

This is an optional sub-section which enables a more precise date to be recorded from sources such as documentary evidence, inscriptions, radiocarbon dates, and dendrochronological dates.

### 2.4.4.1 Date

The scientific or absolute date associated with the monument or site, e.g., 1580–1410 Cal BC (HAR-1234).
*(Alphanumeric, Unique, Mandatory)*

### 2.4.4.2 Method

This indicates the method by which the date was derived, e.g., Carbon 14, dendrochronology. A controlled vocabulary is desirable.
*(Alphanumeric, Unique, Mandatory)*

### 2.5 Physical Condition

This section is used to record the physical condition of the monument or site and the date of an assessment. It is optional and can be repeated. It may be useful for the continued assessment of the management of the monument or site to maintain entries in this section over time. This will enable damage or deterioration to be logged. It may also be necessary to include additional fields to record management details, depending on the functions of the recording organisation.

### 2.5.1 Condition

This field records the physical integrity of the monument or site, e.g., intact, destroyed, restored, unknown, etc. A controlled vocabulary is desirable.
*(Alphanumeric, Unique, Mandatory)*

### 2.5.2 Date Condition Assessed

The date on which the condition was assessed. This field is optional because many condition reports in the past may not have been dated. Use of the ISO standard for date is recommended, e.g., 1994-10-27.
*(Alphanumeric, Unique, Optional)*

### 2.6 Designation/Protection Status

This is an optional section allowing for a statement on whether the monument or site is designated or protected and, if so, the type of designation or protection and the date at which it was granted. This section can be repeated.

### 2.6.1 Type of Designation or Protection

This denotes the designation or protection category. A controlled vocabulary is desirable, e.g., municipal, provincial state, scheduled monument, world heritage site.
*(Alphanumeric, Unique, Mandatory)*

### 2.6.2 Date of Designation or Protection

The date on which the designation or protection was legally granted. Use of the ISO standard for date is recommended, e.g., 1992-11-27.
*(Alphanumeric, Unique, Optional)*

**2.6.3** **Reference Number**

This records the designation or protection reference number, e.g., SSS147.
*(Alphanumeric, Unique, Optional)*

**2.6.4** **Originator of Reference**

The name of the individual or organisation responsible for the reference number, e.g., National Museums Department. This field is mandatory if a reference number is used.
*(Alphanumeric, Unique, Optional)*

**2.7** **Archaeological Summary**

This optional section enables a brief free-text description of the monument or site.
*(Alphanumeric, Unique, Optional)*

# Object ID

## 1.0 Object ID Categories

### 1.1 Photographs
Photographs are of vital importance in identifying and recovering stolen objects. In addition to overall views, close-ups of inscriptions, markings, damage, and repairs should be taken (see **Distinguishing Features**).

### 1.2 Type of Object
**Type of Object** is a term or short descriptive phrase that describes the object (e.g., mask, warrior ear ornament). When implementing Object ID on an automated system it is advisable to be able to retrieve this information at a minimum of two levels (for example, *Level 1*: pottery, *Level 2*: portrait head jar).

### 1.3 Measurements
The size and/or weight of an object, including the unit of measurement (e.g., 30.5 cm by 30.5 cm by 76 cm).

### 1.4 Materials & Techniques
The materials, manufacturing techniques, processes, or methods used to create an object.

### 1.5 Inscriptions & Markings
Identifying markings or inscriptions found on, or applied to, the object (e.g., signature, dedication, title, maker's marks, purity marks, property marks).

### 1.6 Date or Period
An indication of the age of the object. This can be a date or date range (e.g., 1872, 1527–1580) or a cultural period (e.g., Late Bronze Age).

### 1.7 Maker
The name of the maker of an object. This may be a known individual (e.g., Thomas Tompion), a company (e.g., Tiffany), or a cultural group (e.g., Hopi).

**1.8    Subject**
That which is pictured in, or represented by, the object (e.g., landscape, battle, woman holding child).

**1.9    Title**
The title assigned to an object, either at the time of its creation or at a later date (e.g., *The Scream*).

**1.10    Distinguishing Features**
Any features on the object that could uniquely identify it (e.g., damage, repairs, or defects introduced in the manufacturing process).

**1.11    Description**
A short textual description of the object created using information from the above categories. It can include any additional information that helps to identify the object (e.g., colour and shape of the object, where the object was made).

**2.0    Recommended Additional Categories**
Five of the categories of information not selected for Object ID because there was no clear consensus in favor of their inclusion were, however, regarded as being important by a large majority of respondents in at least four of the six communities surveyed. It is recommended that those developing automated documentation systems consider including these categories.

**2.1    Object ID Number**
A numeric or alphanumeric identifier, as used in many museums (sometimes applied to the object itself).

**2.2    Related Written Material**
References, including citations, to other written material related to an object (e.g., published catalogues, articles, condition reports).

**2.3    Place of Origin/Discovery**
The place from which an object originated and/or the location at which it was discovered (e.g., the place it was made, or the archaeological site at which it was discovered).

**2.4    Cross Reference to Related Objects**
An indication that an object is related to a number of others (e.g., one of a pair, part of a dinner service).

**2.5    Date Documented**
The date on which the description of the object was made.

# Object ID
## Checklist

☐ **Take Photographs**
Photographs are of vital importance in identifying and recovering stolen objects.
In addition to overall views, take close-ups of inscriptions, markings, and any dam-
age and repairs. If possible, include a scale or object of known size in the image.

☐ **Answer These Questions**

### Type of Object
What type of object is it (e.g., *painting, sculpture, clock, mask*)?

### Materials and Techniques
What materials is the object made of (e.g., *brass, wood, oil on canvas*)? How
was it made (e.g., *carved, cast, etched*)?

### Measurements
What is the size and/or weight of the object? Specify which unit of measurement is being used (e.g., cm., in.) and to which dimension the measurement
refers (e.g., height, width, depth).

### Inscriptions and Markings
Are there any identifying markings, numbers or inscriptions on the object (e.g.,
a signature, dedication, title, maker's marks, purity marks, property marks)?

### Distinguishing Features
Does the object have any physical characteristics that could help to identify it
(e.g., damage, repairs, or manufacturing defects)?

### Title
Does the object have a title by which it is known and might be identified
(e.g., *The Scream*)?

### Subject
What is pictured or represented (e.g., *landscape, battle, woman holding child*)?

**Date or Period**
When was the object made (e.g., *1893, early 17th century, Late Bronze Age*)?

**Maker**
Do you know who made the object? This may be the name of a known individual (e.g., *Thomas Tompion*), a company (e.g., *Tiffany*), or cultural group (e.g., *Hopi*).

☐ **Write a Short Description**
This can also include any additional information which helps to identify the object (e.g., colour and shape of the object, where it was made).

☐ **Keep it Secure**
Having documented the object, keep this information in a safe place.

# Theoretical Framework of the Core Data Standard for Archaeological Sites and Monuments (with Glossary of Terms)

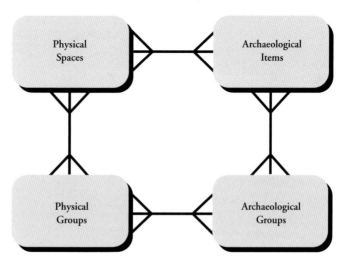

*Figure 4. Schematic representation of the theoretical framework*

## Theoretical Framework Elements

The core data standard has been devised within a theoretical framework consisting of four elements:

- **Archaeological Item**

  An archaeological item is a fundamental piece of archaeology with which the database is concerned. Items could be artefacts like pot sherds or stone tools; ecofacts like seeds or bones; constructional elements like walls or post-holes; or monuments like temples or dwellings. The scale of the archaeological item and the attributes recorded for it will be determined by the purpose of the database.

- **Archaeological Group**

  An archaeological group is a collection of archaeological items which form higher level constructs. These groupings of items have greater interpretative or descriptive power than the individual items. Examples would include the set of flint flakes, tools, and the core that form a flint nodule after refitting, or the sherds that form a ceramic vessel. Dissimilar objects may also be grouped, such as the set of constructional (mound, stone chamber, and ditch), artefactual (jewellery, stone tools, and ceramics) and ecofactual (skeletal remains, pollen, and buried soil) archaeological items.

- **Physical Space**

  A physical space is a division of the real world within which archaeological items are found. They can be of any size or shape and can be defined in any manner appropriate to the archaeology and task. For example, the physical spaces used in an excavation record would be the contexts excavated and in a site inventory they might be land parcels or areas of land with statutory protection. Physical spaces may not overlap. Implementational considerations, especially when concerned with data that are imprecise or inaccurate, may seem to require that this rule is relaxed. It is recommended, however, that this is done only in extreme cases.

- **Physical Group**

  A physical group is a collection of physical spaces which form larger spaces within which archaeological items and groups may occur. Examples would include the areas of land that constitute a statutorily protected monument, or the group of excavation levels or contexts which make up a ditch and its fill. They need not be contiguous, as for instance where parts of a linear feature are divided by modern intrusions which totally destroy the archaeology.

The relationships between the different elements are governed by certain rules as follows:

- An archaeological item will exist in one or more physical space.
- An archaeological item may exist on its own or as part of an archaeological group or groups.
- Physical spaces should not overlap with other physical spaces, although on rare occasions they may appear to, where data are imprecise or inaccurate.

## Glossary

### Cadastral
A system for allocating reference numbers to blocks of land.

### Data Structure
A formal arrangement of elements of data in fields which specify the expressions and format for recording data.

**Designated Site**
A site which has been identified as having a particular status by an organisation; it does not imply any legal protection.

**Free Text**
A text field, without a controlled vocabulary, which can be any length that is supported by the information system in use.

**ISO**
International Organisation for Standardisation; an international organisation charged with developing standards for the international exchange of information.

**Locality**
Any named inhabited area; used in the core data standard for postal address where it is not the name of a town or city.

**Mandatory**
Information that must be supplied ("unknown" may be an acceptable entry). In the core data standard, core sections are mandatory. Within sections that are optional, some sub-sections are mandatory if that section is used.

**Monument**
A site with standing structural elements; site is the more inclusive term.

**Originator of Reference**
Used throughout the core data standard to identify individuals or organisations which are the source of references.

**Parent–Child Relationship**
A hierarchical relationship between two items of data. The "parent" is one level above the "child." For a parent–child relationship, both the "parent" and the "child" must exist.

**Provenance**
The place of origin of an object or record, or the documentation of the history of origin and transfer of objects or records. In North America the alternative spelling "provenience" is used to distinguish the former meaning.

**Qualifier**
A term which modifies the principal term, providing additional information.

**Site**
Any place or set of remains so designated by an individual or organisation; usually meets formal criteria for such designation.

**Site Category**
A general classification system based on the site function. It includes one or more site types with a common function.

**Site Type**
A classification system that describes the function of the site. It is a more specific term than site category.

**Topology**
The properties of a geometrical figure.

**Unique**
Used in the core data standard to refer to a piece of discrete information that is expressed in characters (i.e., words or letters), numbers, or a combination. Different pieces of discrete information are contained in separate, repeating fields.

1 *Compendium of Basic Texts of the Council of Europe in the Field of Cultural Heritage,* CC-PAT (96) 58, 11.

2 Convention for the Protection of the Architectural Heritage of Europe, Granada, 3.X.1985, Council of Europe Treaties ETS No. 121.

3 European Convention for the Protection of the Archaeological Heritage of Europe (revised), Valletta, 16.I.1992, Council of Europe Treaties ETS No. 143.

4 Council of Europe, Cultural Heritage Division, CC-PAT (93) 131, 2.

5 *Ibid.*

6 Final Act of the Diplomatic Conference for the Adoption of the Draft UNIDROIT Convention on the International Return of Stolen or Illegally Exported Cultural Objects, Rome, Ministerio degli Affari Esteri, June 24, 1995.

7 *Architectural Heritage: Inventory and Documentation Methods in Europe.* Proceedings of a European colloquy organized by the Council of Europe and the French Ministry for Education and Culture—Direction du patrimoine, Nantes, October 28–31, 1992. Strasbourg: Council of Europe, 1993, 12.

8 See Bold, J. and Grant, S. "Contingent Boundaries—The Channel Tunnel Rail Link Considered as an Architectural Ensemble," *Transactions of the Ancient Monuments Society,* vol. 41, 1997, 59–73.

9 Larsen 1992.

10 The findings of the questionnaire surveys carried out since then have strongly endorsed this recommendation. Ninety-eight percent of customs agencies, 97 percent of cultural heritage organisations (supplementary survey), 96 percent of appraisers, 95 percent of law-enforcement agencies (supplementary survey), and 88 percent of the art trade have approved it.

*Architectural Heritage: Inventory and Documentation Methods in Europe.* Proceedings of a European colloquy organized by the Council of Europe and the French Ministry for Education and Culture—Direction du patrimoine, Nantes, October 28–31, 1992. Strasbourg: Council of Europe, 1993.

*Architectural Heritage, New Technologies in Documentation.* Proceedings of a roundtable organised by the Council of Europe and the Royal Commission on the Historical Monuments of England, London, November 7–10, 1989. Strasbourg: Council of Europe, 1990.

Askerud, P. and Clément, E. *Preventing the Illicit Traffic in Cultural Property: A Resource Handbook for the Implementation of the 1970 UNESCO Convention.* Paris: UNESCO, 1997.

Bold, J. "Patrimoine Architectural: Cooperation de Centres de Documentation". *Villes, Architectures, Metiers: Banques de Données des Savoir-Faire.* Marseille: Atelier du Patrimoine, 1990, 4-7.

Bold, J. *Technical Assistance for a Computerised Heritage Documentation Centre in Malta.* Architectural Heritage No. 23, Strasbourg: Council of Europe, 1992.

Bold, J. and Grant, S. "Contingent Boundaries—The Channel Tunnel Rail Link Considered as an Architectural Ensemble". *Transactions of the Ancient Monuments Society,* vol. 41, 1997, 59-73.

Chenhall, R.G., and Homulos, P. "Museum Data Standards". *Museum,* vol. 314, 1978, 205–212.

*Compendium of Basic Texts of the Council of Europe in the Field of Cultural Heritage,* CC-PAT (96) 58, provisional version, Strasbourg: Council of Europe, 1996. Convention for the Protection of the Architectural Heritage of Europe, Granada, 3.X.1985, Council of Europe Treaties ETS No. 121.

Convention for the Protection of the Archaeological Heritage of Europe (revised), Valletta, 16.I.1992, Council of Europe Treaties ETS No. 143.

*Core Data Index to Historic Buildings and Monuments of the Architectural Heritage.* Recommendation R (95) 3 of the Committee of Ministers of the Council of Europe to member states on co-ordinating documentation methods and systems related to historic buildings and monuments of the architectural heritage. Strasbourg: Council of Europe, 1995.

Council of Europe, Cultural Heritage Division, CC-PAT (93) 131, 2. (Report on Prague meeting on threats to the movable heritage in central and eastern Europe.)

Final Act of the Diplomatic Conference for the Adoption of the Draft UNIDROIT Convention on the International Return of Stolen or Illegally Exported Cultural Objects, Rome, Ministerio degli Affari Esteri, June 24, 1995.

Getty Art History Information Program and International Council of Museums International Documentation Committee. *Developments in International Museum and Cultural Heritage Information Standards.* Santa Monica: Getty Art History Information Program, 1993.

Grant, A. *Spectrum: The U.K. Museum Documentation Standard.* Cambridge: Museum Documentation Association, 1994.

*Handbook of Standards, Documenting African Collections.* Paris: International Council of Museums, 1996.

Harrison, R., ed. *Manual of Heritage Management.* Oxford: Oxford University Press, 1994.

Holm, S. *Facts and Artifacts: How to Document a Museum Collection.* Cambridge: Museum Documentation Association, 1991.

*Humanities Data Dictionary of the Canadian Heritage Information Network.* Ottawa: Canadian Heritage Information Network, 1993.

*International Guidelines for Museum Object Information: The CIDOC Information Categories.* Paris: International Council of Museums, 1995.

Lang, N. and Stead, S.D. "Sites and Monuments Records in England—Theory and Practice". *Computer Applications and Quantitative Methods in Archaeology,* BAR International Series, 1992, 69–76.

Larsen, C.U., ed. *Sites and Monuments. National Archaeological Records.* Copenhagen: The National Museum of Denmark (DKC), 1992.

Marques, T., ed. *Carta Arqueológica de Portugal.* Lisbon: Secretaria de Estado da Cultura & Instituto Português do Património Arquitectónico e Arqueológico, 1992.

*Minimum Categories for Museum Objects: Proposed Guidelines for an International Standard.* Paris: International Council of Museums, 1994.

*Normes Documentaires (Archéologie)/ Data Standards (Archaeology).* International Council of Museums, International Committee for Documentation (CIDOC), unpublished.

Porter, V. and Thornes, R. *A Guide to the Description of Architectural Drawings.* Boston: G. K. Hall, 1994.

*Protecting Cultural Objects in the Global Information Society* (video). Santa Monica: Getty Information Institute, 1996.

Reilly, P. and Rahtz, S. "Archaeology in the Information Age: A Global Perspective". *One World Archaeology,* vol. 21. London: Routledge, 1992.

Roberts, D. A., ed. *European Museum Documentation Strategies and Standards.* Cambridge: The Museum Documentation Association, 1993.

Ross, S., Moffet, J. and Henderson, J., eds. *Computing for Archaeologists.* Oxford University Committee for Archaeology, Monograph 18, 1991.

Royal Commission on the Historical Monuments of England and the Association of County Archaeological Officers. *Recording England's Past: A Data Standard for the Extended National Archaeological Record.* London: RCHME, 1993.

Royal Commission on the Historical Monuments of England and English Heritage. *Thesaurus of Monument Types: A Standard for Use in Archaeological and Architectural Records.* Swindon: RCHME, 1995.

*Specification for Representation of Dates and Times in Information Interchange.* (ISO 8601: 198S/ ES EN 28601:1992). Geneva: International Organisation for Standardisation, 1988.

Thornes, R. *Protecting Cultural Objects through International Documentation Standards: A Preliminary Survey.* Santa Monica: Getty Art History Information Program, 1995.

Thornes, R. *Protecting Cultural Objects in the Global Information Society: The Making of Object ID.* Santa Monica: Getty Information Institute, 1997.